Your Vegan Kid

The guide to raising a healthy, happy
and compassionate human being

Joanna Draus

Disclaimer: This book details the author's personal experiences with and opinions about a vegan diet. The author is not your healthcare provider. The information in this book is for general information only, and is not intended or implied to be a substitute for professional medical advice, diagnosis or treatment. Please consult with <u>your</u> own physician, pediatrician or healthcare specialist about the suggestions and recommendations made in this book. Before you begin any healthcare program or change your lifestyle in any way, please consult your physician, pediatrician or other licensed healthcare practitioner to ensure that you and your child are in good health and that the examples contained in this book will not harm you. This book provides content related to health issues. As such, use of this book implies your acceptance of this disclaimer.

Your Vegan Kid: The Guide to Raising a Healthy, Happy and Compassionate Human Being

International Standard Book Number (ISBN)
978-83-954787-2-7

For my wonderful kids Weronika, Igor, and Olaf. I would never be the person I am if it weren't for you.

All my love,
Mom

Contents

Preface

First of all, I would like to congratulate you, because if you are reading this book, I assume you are thinking about raising your child vegan or (even better) you are already doing so. Moreover, you are looking for information, since you want to make well-informed choices concerning your kid. You must also be a nonconformist and a responsible parent who cares about her/his child's health, or the environment, or animal welfare, or all of the above. These are even more reasons to be proud of yourself.

In our digitally connected society, we are flooded with information every single day; here, I offer the information I wish I could have found in one convenient place when I began my journey of raising vegan children. The aim of this book is to encourage and help all parents who think about or are already raising their children vegan. In this book, I express my personal opinions based on both my experience and my studies. I am not a scientist – I am a mother of three vegan kids (12-year-old twin sons and a 27-year-old daughter) who happened to have time, curiosity and resources to learn about plant-based nutrition and vegan child-raising. There are still few vegan parents (and kids for that matter), and there is great social prejudice and pressure against those who are vegan. I have been confronting it for 27 years now, ever since I decided to raise my first child vegetarian, and then the angle changed 13 years ago, when I became pregnant with twins and decided to raise them vegan. And I have talked to many parents about the obstacles and problems they encountered on their way to raise their kids vegan. The intention of this book is to help those who are dealing with those same obstacles and problems now.

Every single day we make choices. We make them for ourselves, and maybe even more importantly, we make them for our children. There is no such a thing as "not making a choice" or "a neutral choice." If, for example, you raise your kid the way you were raised (or the way your mother tells you to), you are also making a choice. The same goes for following your more experienced friends' or even your doctor's advice. And of course, it also goes for me – I'm just sharing my thoughts and experiences with you here. But you need to do whatever your mind and heart dictate, since at the end of a day, you are your child's parent and you are responsible for his or her well-being. I wrote this book because I strongly believe veganism is the ultimate way to raise a truly healthy, happy and compassionate human being, and I want to share the knowledge I've gained so I can help other parents pursue this wonderful goal.

Introduction – my story

Though it took me many years before I committed to a vegan life, I can trace my veganism back to an early experience: when I was three years old, I asked my parents what the meat on my plate was. They said it was a cow, and I cried a lot when I learned this. I can still remember the feeling of shock, terror and disgust. My parents explained to me that it was "a natural order of things" and that I needed it "to be healthy and grow strong," but still, it didn't seem right to me. Of course, they believed it, and with time, I believed it, too. There was not much choice when I was a small child – my mother would usually prepare a main dish consisting of potatoes or groats, red meat and some vegetables. And I can still remember her saying: "You can leave the veggies, but you should eat up your meat." Since I hated meat, I desperately tried to avoid eating it. I used to feed it to our dogs under the table unnoticed. I also had some hiding places for my uneaten meat – like the one in a flowerpot under the roots of a big plant we had. I was so desperate that I even remember pretending to chew on my meat and then stuffing it into my pockets when nobody was looking, in order to throw it away in the toilet.

My parents also insisted on my drinking milk. When I started to attend kindergarten and then elementary school, there was an obligatory milk drinking program for all the students. Of course, in 1970s Poland, nobody had heard about food allergies and cow's milk was considered to be what we call a "super food" nowadays. However, I was very allergic to cow's milk – even its smell made me feel sick. When I drank milk, it caused phlegm production in my upper respiratory tract and constant nasal congestion. But whenever I got sick, my parents made me drink hot milk with honey in a good faith, because it was also traditionally believed to be a cure-all. I soon developed an allergy to honey as well. (These days I don't eat it, of course, but still my throat gets sore just at its smell!) So, obviously, I got even sicker each time. I remember lying in bed and envying my friends who played outside. My parents worried about me a lot. I got sick very often and for long periods of time. My parents also labeled me a poor eater and worried about my low weight. They brought me to different doctors, but apart from administering lots of unnecessary medication and continuing with a diet full of meat and milk, they had no advice whatsoever.

My health started to improve gradually when I was about nine years old, thanks to two factors. The first was the very old-school pediatrician my parents found, who told them to stop medicating me with antibiotics, and insisted on administering natural cures, such as garlic, onion, and linden infusions. He also understood the role of fresh fruits in a diet. Secondly, at this time, I was big enough to insist on my choices, and my diet was shifting towards a healthier one. I refused to drink cow's milk and preferred fish and poultry to red meat. Within a few years, another very important thing happened – my father met a vegetarian man (a rare breed in Poland in the 1980s), and they became friends. Under his friend's influence, my dad stopped eating meat and poultry. He even gave me a book on vegetarianism, which I did not read, since I was a rebel. Obviously, he didn't cook for himself (it was still Poland of the 80s), and so my mom was forced to shift her cuisine towards a vegetarian one, or she served two different meals sometimes. I used to eat what my father had. But still, I was too lazy to cook for myself. I became pickier about my mother's cuisine, but it suited me to have everything prepared for me. I also became a great eater, and I still am – I enjoy eating foods that I like. I am still thin and so are all my children, despite their eating a lot. I believe it is thanks to our genetic metabolism and our vegan diet that is rich in fiber.

The next big change in my diet took place when I got pregnant. First, I moved from my parents' house to live with my fiancé. I tried to cook some traditional dishes that we both used to eat. But what seemed so easy and natural to my mother was not easy at all for me. Though I had been eating meat, fish and poultry and was conscious that they were the bodies of dead animals, I did not give it much thought. It was not a subject I liked to contemplate—on the contrary, I tried to ignore it and therefore would never cook them myself.

The turning point came when I bought a chicken and tried to cook a broth with it. While it was easy to peel and cut vegetables, it was really difficult for me to cut the chicken. I could no longer ignore the fact that it had flesh, bones, tendons, and veins full of blood – very similar to the ones found in a human body. I still remember fighting to fit the dead bird inside the pot – its feet with claws kept sticking out. I was doing my best to put them inside with a fork because I could not touch them with my bare hands, since they seemed disgusting. This was the one and only meat dish I have ever cooked. I still ate some meat, poultry and fish, if somebody else prepared them for me, but I knew I could not and did not want to do it myself.

And then during my pregnancy, many childhood memories came back. And of course, whenever I recalled any trauma, I vowed not to do the same thing to my child. One of the first things that came to my mind was my realization that meat was dead animal flesh. I was still omnivorous, though consuming relatively little meat, fish and poultry or other animal products. My daughter was born, and she was exclusively breastfed for the first five months of her life. During these months I became anxious to find a solution. I didn't want my daughter to cry when she eventually learned that we eat dead animals' corpses. It was 1993 and the Internet still wasn't an option. Therefore, I looked for books... and rediscovered that dusty and still unread book my father gave me. It was written by a deceased Polish philosopher and propagator of vegetarianism, Maria Grodecka, and is called "Zmierzch Świadomości Łowcy," which means "A Twilight of the Hunter's Consciousness" (the book never got translated into other languages). It was mainly of a philosophical and ethical nature, but still I found the answers to all my questions and doubts in just one chapter. In this chapter, called "Super Baby," the author reassured me and confirmed all my gut feelings when she said that vegetarian kids can grow up healthy – and even healthier than their non-vegetarian contemporaries. I cannot describe the relief and bliss I felt when I read it. Once I got ahold of this book, I couldn't stop reading it – I didn't sleep and finished it by sunrise. The next day, I announced to my partner and father of my daughter: "Our daughter and I will be vegetarian from now on. Here is the book you might want to read. Let me know when you make up your mind." Simple as that, I left him the book. After the next two or three days, he said he was on board with my decision.

I remember very strong opposition from both my and my partner's families when we announced that not only we, but also our daughter, would be vegetarian. The idea was mine, but he had my back. The open criticism and attempts to undermine our decision on every occasion lasted for around two years and then gradually ceased. I believe three factors played an important role in this: first, all the family saw that our daughter was a healthy growing child; second, we had demonstrated steadfastness in our decision; and third, they just got used to it and found more interesting, newer things to comment upon.

By the time my daughter was three months old, we had become vegetarian. Having a vegetarian newborn in Poland in 1993 was not easy. The typical Polish diet at the time consisted of cow's milk with cereal for breakfast; soup based on chicken or meat broth as the first course; and potatoes, meat or fish and some vegetables as the second course for the main meal; and then cheese or ham sandwiches for supper. All the doctors and my family members were against my choice. Milk and meat were still seen as an essential part of a healthy diet. But I kept going, despite all the fears and concerns (even my own). Though she was growing up healthy, I was not entirely sure of my decision until she was two-and-a-half years old. One day, my daughter and I went shopping in a supermarket. We were walking through the aisles holding hands. At some point, I felt her fingernails piercing into my palm and when I looked down, I saw her eyes brimming with tears, and she screamed to me, "Mom, there are hens with their heads chopped off, let's get out of here!" And then I felt deep relief and I thought I had done a good job as her mother — after all, I spared her the shock and trauma that I went through as a child. And seeing how profound her reaction was to other people's dietary practices, I was very proud and happy that they weren't ours. At this early point, I had never told her about animal slaughter or abuse, since I believed she was too small and sensitive at the time. And her father, who was on board with me, would not do so either. But she was a smart kid and somehow figured it out herself.

When she was three years old, we went on vacation in the countryside as a group of three mothers and three daughters all around the same age. We had a great time together, and one night we set a campfire and had traditional campfire Polish foods. We buried some potatoes in ashes, and we had some on-the-stick foods, like apples and bread, and sausages for the meat eaters (there were no plant-based sausages at the time). At one point, my daughter came to ask me if she could try the campfire sausage, and she said: "Mom, it smells so good." I said: "Yes, go ahead." And after some time, she came back to me and she said: "Mom, it smelled and tasted really good, it is just a pity, we have to harm the animals to get it." The only thing I could think to do at the time was to hug her and to say, "I know." This was the first and the last time she has ever expressed any interest in meat eating.

Around the same time that my toddler daughter saw the headless chickens in the market, my mother made a surprising change. Having seen her granddaughter growing healthily for the first two years of her life on an ovo-vegetarian diet, she became convinced she should become a vegetarian too – and she still is after 24 years! Her decision also impacted my younger siblings. My younger brother ate vegetarian for a few years; then he stopped and had to confront his high cholesterol level and obesity after a few years. My younger sister hasn't eaten any meat or poultry since then, and I hope she will eventually become vegan.

My mother's transition didn't come out of the blue, however. Growing up, she had been fed a standard Polish diet consisting largely of animal products. In college, she studied the food industry and agro-food processing. When she was 20 years old, she had to do an internship in a slaughterhouse for six weeks. She can still remember how much she was traumatized by it. She said the students saw the slaughterhouse production line only once, on the first day, and some of them got sick because of the sights and smells during their visit. Then they were sent to the other factory, where they packed cucumbers into jars for the rest of their "slaughterhouse internship," since their professors knew they couldn't take more. My mother said that when she came back home, she couldn't touch meat for over a year.

Since my daughter, who was exclusively breastfed, was lactose-intolerant, I introduced only plant-based foods into her diet when she was six months old, and then eggs and butter when she was one year old. She started to consume other dairy products in small quantities when she was eight. She was vegetarian until she was 23 years old, when she decided to go vegan. I went vegan in 2004, and my twin sons born in 2007 have always been vegan.

1 Why vegan?

Health (and happiness)

If you are reading this book, you are probably already aware of the health benefits of the plant-based diet. But maybe you are still hesitating over whether veganism is appropriate for babies and children. My nutritional expertise is mainly practical – it comes from raising one vegetarian and then two vegan kids. In addition to gaining expertise through my personal experience, I earned a Plant-Based Nutrition Certificate from eCornell University and the T. Colin Campbell Center for Nutrition Studies, and I am deeply convinced that whole food veganism is the best diet for a human being at any stage of life.

When looking for evidence of the plant-based diet's benefits, you should keep in mind that there is big money involved in lobbying and propaganda for the animal farming industry, which has been promoting consumption of their products since the 1950s. From then until now, it has managed to instill many scientifically unsupported notions into the public consciousness. The most popular myths are the ones about protein and calcium. The protein myth consists of the notion that humans should consume animal foods, since they are richer in proteins than plant-based ones. While the latter is true, there is overwhelming and growing evidence that it is the oversupply of protein that causes most of the so-called civilization diseases, such as obesity, high blood pressure, diabetes, heart disease and cancer. As for calcium, we have been told for decades that we have to consume dairy in order to provide our bodies with a sufficient calcium supply. Yet in light of current research, it is clear that our bodies do not absorb calcium from the dairy products we consume. There are large-scale studies showing that people who consume cow's milk are not only not at lesser risk for osteoporosis, but are at greater risk for bone fractures. Apart from that, cow's milk is one of the most dangerous carcinogens and the most reported allergen in the world.

Strangely enough, nobody asks parents whose children consume a standard Western diet about how nutritious it is or about possible dietary deficiencies, whereas upon learning that your child is vegan, non-vegan family members, friends, health practitioners and even complete strangers start voicing their concerns. You can easily see the irony here – especially considering their dietary practices and the fact that omnivorous children get sick and sometimes lack essential nutrients. (Vegan children are still so rare that there are no comparative studies about them.)

While there is massive and constantly growing evidence that animal-based foods are harmful for humans, studies on plant-based nutrition are still scarce. If you want to look for scientific proof, I recommend checking out The China Study, one of the most comprehensive and largest nutrition studies so far. (Also have a look at the "Further reading" chapter at the end of this book.)

If you check the World Health Organization website for information on children's nutrition, you can find the following information under Children's Diet/General Information:

> Currently there is no dietary recommendation of global utility available for children and adolescents. However, individuals and populations are advised to:
> - increase the consumption of fruit and vegetables, as well as legumes, whole grains and nuts;

- limit the energy intake from total fats and shift fat consumption away from saturated fats to unsaturated fats;
- limit the intake of sugars.

The Physicians Committee for Responsible Medicine says, "A plant-based diet is a healthful choice at every stage of life, including pregnancy and breastfeeding." The Vegan Society says on its website, "Both the British Dietetic Association and the American Academy of Nutrition and Dietetics recognize that a well-planned vegan diet follows healthy eating guidelines and contains all the nutrients that our bodies need and is suitable for every age and stage of life."

Health and happiness are inextricably linked. I strongly believe that our state of mind depends on our health and vice versa. Ancient Romans had the saying: "Mens sana in corpore sano," which translates as "a healthy mind in a healthy body." Many cases of behavioral disorders in children can be linked to allergies, food intolerances, food contamination, or an unbalanced diet — which means that shifting to a healthier diet can reduce these symptoms. We don't have to expect suffering from conditions such as obesity, heart disease, chronic fatigue, or cancer, all of which are diet-related, when it is within our power to provide our bodies with the best nutrition available.

Each cell of our bodies is built from the ingredients we provide, and therefore our body's condition depends on nutrition. There are many conditions we cannot control, such as the air we breathe, the noise surrounding us, and sometimes even our stress levels, but we can be in charge of what we eat and what we feed to our children.

Psychology and well-being

While there is a lot of interest in veganism recently, most of it revolves around plant-based recipes or animal welfare, with some talk about the health benefits of the plant-based diet. But still there is little discussion about the health of vegan babies or kids, since they are a whole new generation. And information about how the vegan lifestyle can affect your child's well-being for non-dietary reasons is even scarcer.

I believe we are all born innocent, trusting and loving. Human infants tend to smile at other humans and animals from the time they are born, and when they grow older, they want to cuddle them. And then the family and society destroy that sensitivity and innocence to facilitate our adjustment to social norms and customs. Families want to raise good (meaning obedient) kids. And society wants to raise good (meaning compliant) workers and customers.

Though it is increasingly coming into question, consuming animal products is still a norm of contemporary Western society. I strongly believe it would not be possible to maintain such norms if a whole set of hypocritical societal beliefs and customs had not been inculcated since our early childhood. The manipulation takes place in four main ways: hiding the truth, holding double standards, disguising the truth, and making excuses.

Hiding the truth

Imagine how many people would continue to eat meat if they had to kill the animals themselves. Or imagine how many people would continue to eat dairy or eggs after visiting a factory farming facility. As Sir Paul McCartney said: "If slaughterhouses had glass walls, everyone would be a vegetarian."

And how many people would continue their omnivore diets, if they truly internalized the information that their lifestyle is directly responsible for hunger in the third world and for global warming?

So the truth is out there, but it is mostly hidden. It takes a good amount of determination to find it and then the courage to face it. On the other hand, we are fed such an enormous number of lies daily that it is easy to forget about the truth, especially if taking it in would necessitate a profound change in our behavior.

When it comes to children, I would not encourage anybody to make a trip to a factory farm or to show them any graphic material about it. But it is important to acknowledge that we as a society are feeding our kids not only the animal products, but also the monstrous lies about where this food comes from and how it is obtained.

Double standards

Another question – why in Western culture is it completely unacceptable to eat dogs and cats, while it is considered perfectly normal to eat cows and pigs? It is not because of their intelligence – there are studies showing that pigs share several cognitive capacities with other highly intelligent species such as dogs, chimpanzees, elephants, and dolphins. It is not because they are less good-looking either. All little mammals are cute. What happens to them next is a result of the conditions they live in.

We raise our children to feel that it is good to love animals and respect nature. You do not see parents encouraging their kids to harm cats and dogs; on the contrary, most people say, "Look, how cute!" But still, every day, we teach our children to consume the products of animal death and suffering. And we nevertheless call ourselves "animal lovers" or "environmentalists" and pass on these false labels to our kids.

Our children watch "Peppa Pig" and cuddle with animal-shaped toys when they sleep. And still we serve them animal meat, as if it were a perfectly normal thing to do.

Disguising the truth

Another way the animal farming industry sells its products is to dress them up as something different. I have met many adults who admit they do not enjoy the sight (or smell) of raw meat. Still, they are perfectly happy eating meat if it's prepared by somebody else.

The same is true for our kids. I doubt

children would enjoy eating a steak or chicken wings if they were to see how the meat is chopped off from the animal's body, or had to face the smell and sight of blood, bones, tendons, etc. So instead, we feed our children convenient foods like burgers or "fish fingers," which look and smell tastier than the original "product." Jelly beans are probably the most absurd example of disguising a food's animal origins. Jelly beans come in all forms, colors, flavors and smells – and do not remind us of animals at all. But in the end, they are just a mash of cooked animal bones – which is where gelatin comes from – with such artificial additives as colorings, aromas, and flavors.

The disguise strategy is used not only on the physical level; most animal food marketing is based on it. Unlike film producers, food manufacturers would not lie to us, saying that "no animal was harmed during production." Nowadays even small children know that some products come from animals, so the industry does not deny the products' origins. Instead, they present animal-food production as though it is something good for both the animals and the consumers – I am sure you can recall absurd advertising campaigns in which happy cows are giving children cheese or other milk products, or pictures of smiling piglets advertising pork on the butchers' boards. Animal product advertising is characterized by pastoral, idyllic images of animals – for example, cows and baby calves grazing in green pastures on a sunny day. Often there's a human child in the picture, too. I have just come across a strong lampoon of such advertising practices while watching the "BoJack Horseman" animated series on Netflix (I believe you can also find it on YouTube; it's S02E05 "Chickens"). Animal product advertising cannot be further from the truth – almost of these products come from factory farming, which is not only cruel, but also extremely unpleasant to see, hear and smell.

Making excuses

Sooner or later everybody becomes aware that they are consuming animal products. And we are more or less conscious about the suffering behind it (and I am not only talking about the animal suffering here). Still, our families and our society provide us a whole range of excuses for continuing this lifestyle. (Don't get me wrong, I do not believe they have come up with them – most of these excuses are just products of animal industry propaganda, which results in unquestioned behaviors and habits spread throughout our society.) First, they say that animal products are good or even necessary for our health. Second, they say it is human nature to eat animal products. And finally, they say it is a tradition that you should respect—all lies, just to keep you from changing your habits and beliefs about what is best to eat (and in the end, about what we should spend our money on).

When we are kids, our family feeds us the same kinds of excuses in good faith. They tell us we need to eat meat and drink milk to grow healthy and strong. And since they are simply repeating these beliefs for years or maybe generations, they truly believe in them, and that is why they would go even further and make an emotional cause of it. That is why we hear things like: "Your grandma has cooked this delicious chicken broth for you. You don't want to upset her by refusing to eat it, do you?"

Ecology and ethics

When raising your children, you are not only feeding them and assuring their physical safety, you are also passing on a whole set of values, beliefs and customs. And ultimately you are shaping a new human being, a member of a future society, and a creative component of the future world. If you are raising your child vegan – I commend you! Apart from your child's healthy physical and psychological development, you are making our world a better place.

First, consider the fact that the vegan diet is good not only for vegans, but also for the whole human race. There are two issues here: feeding a growing population and keeping it healthy. A plant-based diet is much more efficient than a diet based on animal products. Here are some numbers: an area of 0.6 hectare can be used to produce either 16,783 kg (37,000 lbs) of plant-based food or 170 kg (375 lbs) of meat. Producing 1 kg (2.2 lbs) of animal protein requires about 100 times more water than producing 1 kg of grain protein. In addition, in factory farming, antibiotics are administered to healthy animals on a daily basis to promote growth and to prevent diseases. Therefore, the plant-based diet not only keeps people healthy, but also addresses land and water depletion and the growing threat of antibiotic resistance.

Second, veganism is the optimal solution as far as our environment is concerned. Animal-based food production not only plays a major role in depleting natural resources such as farm land and water, it also requires significant quantities of nonrenewable fossil fuel energy. And it plays a huge role in the worsening of the greenhouse effect.

And third, it is obviously good for the animals – many pages have been written on animal rights, animal psychology and ethics. It doesn't really matter if you're a cat person or a dog person, or neither, or whether you believe that animals have souls. If you know they are sentient beings, it should be obvious to you that animals shouldn't suffer and be killed to satisfy our palates.

So if you decide to raise your child vegan, you are taking care not only about his or her healthy body and mind – you are also taking responsibility and care about other beings on our planet. You are also passing on these humanitarian and ecological values and thus making sure they influence future generations.

2   Phases of a child's life

Pregnancy and breastfeeding

If you are starting from zero – that is, ideally, before you got pregnant – great work! Just make sure to eat the whole food plant-based diet and supplement B12 yourself before and throughout your pregnancy and breastfeeding. However, it is never too late to start your journey on the healthy vegan road. You can change your diet and your life at any point.

Remember that you share with your baby everything you eat and drink during pregnancy and breastfeeding. So if you decide to eat a healthy, whole food plant-based diet, this is what you provide your child with. And on the other hand, you spare your child everything that you avoid during this period — for example, dioxins, which are highly concentrated in animal products, can only be eliminated from human bodies via the placenta and breast milk. Studies show that breast milk of vegan women is much less likely to contain contaminants than that of non-vegans.

Moreover, taste preferences and habits are shaped very early in life – in the mother's womb, during breastfeeding, and in the first years of life. The kids whose mothers consume unhealthy foods during pregnancy and breastfeeding may crave these foods at very early stages of life. To illustrate this with the most extreme example: think about the mothers using substances – their children will develop craving or even addiction while still in their bellies. The same goes for sugar or cow's milk products, which also are addictive to some extent.

Everything you eat during pregnancy and breastfeeding is digested and released into your bloodstream and then into the amniotic fluid or breast milk. Moreover, both amniotic fluid and breast milk are to some extent flavored by the food you consume. For these reasons, it's not only a question of providing your kid with all the nutrition she or he needs, but also of developing your child's future taste and food preferences.

The benefits of breastfeeding cannot be overstated for health, psychological and practical reasons. I breastfed my children for as long as I could: my daughter for over three years and my twin sons for 13 months. And I encourage everyone to breastfeed your baby exclusively and on demand for at least the first six months (no bottle even with water during this period). Your milk is the best source of nutrition for your baby and it is perfectly tailored to suit her or his needs. It also provides efficient antibodies, so there is no need to stop breastfeeding if you come down with an infection. Breastfeeding also helps both of you bond in a unique way. And finally, it's so much easier and more practical to breastfeed your baby than to give it a bottle. Your milk is always there, at the perfect temperature. Its density, quantity, and even composition is always up-to-date with your baby's needs. You don't have to buy a baby formula (including looking for a plant-based one), you don't have to buy and then sterilize bottles and nipples, and then carry them along with you. You don't have to wake up in the middle of the night to prepare and warm up the formula. You just wake up and give a breast to your baby – even if you are half-asleep.

And since it is so very important, if you encounter any difficulties when breastfeeding your baby, I strongly recommend that you seek help from a lactation consultant, a breastfeeding mothers' support group, or anyone who can be of help at this stage.

Baby

Ideally, you exclusively breastfeed your baby for the first six months of his or her life and then gradually introduce some solid foods while breastfeeding at least until your child is one year old. Breastfeeding until they are two or three years old would be the best.

While this is a perfect scenario, I know this is not always possible. I managed to achieve it with my daughter, and I breastfed her until she was over three years old, whereas with my twin sons it turned out to be much more challenging, since one of them constantly refused to drink from my breast. Despite my previous experience in breastfeeding and the help of at least three lactation consultants, I finally gave up and started to give him my milk in the bottle and complement it with a plant-based formula when he was one and a half months old. Meanwhile, his brother was perfectly happy and growing faster exclusively breastfed. Because of this atypical twin situation, I started to introduce solid foods into their diet very early — when they were four-and-a-half months old. But I still managed to feed both boys my milk until they were 13 months old.

If you are transitioning to veganism when your child is a baby, it shouldn't present any difficulties at this stage of his or her life, especially if you are exclusively breastfeeding. (As I mentioned in the Introduction, this is when I transitioned from the omni diet to vegetarianism 27 years ago.)

I hope that you can wait to give your child solid foods until they are six months old. What to start with? I recommend a mash of organic foods (or "ecological" or "bio[logical]" as they are also known) for starters. I'm not saying that vegans should eat only organically grown foods, but I believe that it would be best to keep your baby's diet organic for the first year. These can be fresh, steamed or cooked fruits and vegetables depending on the season. My daughter's first solids were grated organic apples. My sons' first were mashed organic avocados.

Then I would add cooked whole grains to the baby's diet. It is best to avoid gluten in the first year of a baby's life. It is important to serve whole grains, because they contain much more nutrients and fiber than the highly processed ones. I still remember when I was leading a support group for breastfeeding mothers in the early 90s. One of the moms started by introducing white rice to her daughter's diet (her partner was Japanese, and therefore they wanted their child to get acquainted with this staple Japanese food first). The little girl enjoyed her rice so much, that she ate two and a half servings the very first time. And then she couldn't poop for three days.

I wouldn't introduce more than one new food every day or every other day for several reasons. First, your baby's body needs to get used to digesting each of them. Second, I believe it is good for the baby to learn each food's taste and texture. And third, this way you can make sure your baby doesn't show any adverse or allergic reaction to the new foods, and if he or she did, you would easily be able to identify which food caused it. (Note that if your child seems to be allergic to any food that wasn't organically grown, sometimes the reaction can be caused by the artificial chemicals – pesticides or insecticides present in it – and not to the food itself. So I would wait for about two weeks and then try to reintroduce the same food, but this time organically grown, if available, to determine the source of the allergic reaction.)

As far as the solid food's consistency is

concerned, you should prepare it according to your baby's teething (please keep in mind that babies' gums become hard much sooner than you can see actual teeth) and their willingness to try the new foods. You can blend them to a smooth pulp, you can grate them or mash them with a fork. Most babies love finger foods, but of course you have to supervise them to make sure they don't choke on them.

As you expand your child's menu, you can start serving more "complex" dishes like vegetable broth, fruits with cereals, and vegetables with whole grains. Please note that salt and any other additives are unnecessary, but you can add a dash of cold-pressed oil just before serving.

At the end of the first year of your child's life (around the ninth month), you can start introducing more foods, such as seeds, nuts and beans. Just remember to do it gradually and one by one, since some of them, especially nuts, can cause an allergic reaction and are harder to digest. You can start to introduce dry ground seeds and nuts by adding a teaspoon of one type to your child's meal. Or you can soak them overnight and then blend them with other foods. As far as beans are concerned, you can start by introducing the bean sprouts or cooked beans in small quantities.

Nowadays there are lots of ready-made vegan and organic baby foods available, but I strongly recommend preparing the food for your child at home. Ready-made foods, even if they don't contain any preservatives, are pasteurized and sometimes spend a long time on the shelf, and thus may have little nutritional value.

I hope you can still breastfeed your baby after introducing solid foods – even once a day is great. However, if your baby will no longer take the breast after completion of first year of life, I believe there is no reason to keep feeding her or him formula (even plant-based ones resemble the periodic table of chemical elements more than actual food). Instead, at this stage, I would opt for water and a variety of organic plant-based milks. You just need to read the ingredients list and make sure that they don't contain any unnecessary ingredients such as sugar and preservatives. They should contain just whole grains or nuts, water, and sometimes sea salt.

Toddler

At the beginning of your child's second year, they should start to eat whatever other family members eat, assuming that your family eats healthy, vegan, and not very hot dishes.

In the early stages of life, your baby takes everything for granted. If there's only healthy plant-based food in your fridge, pantry and on your table (and I hope this is the case for you), your child will see this as obvious and natural. But let's say you go visit your parents or your in-laws or some non-vegan friends and there are some non-vegan foods on the table. Your child will most likely want to try them, so now it's decision time for you. You can either say: "Sure, go ahead." Or you can say: "I'm sorry, but we don't eat this, please try something else."

I can understand the reasons to go for the first option. It's nice to respect your kid's choices and opinions. But it also has its drawbacks: it's likely that your kid will find the non-vegan foods tasty. — Not because they are good for her, but simply because the food is probably highly processed and will please her taste buds in an artificial way. Let's say a kid raised on a healthy plant-based diet tries marshmallows or a regular milk chocolate bar for the very first time. They will probably like it and may develop a sweet tooth. And of course, it won't help to meet their nutritional needs. Moreover, if your kid and your family or friends notice the exception you made (and believe me, they will), on the next occasion they will expect you to do the same.

I personally always went for the no-exceptions option at the early stage of my kids' lives. Why? First, because I didn't want my kids to eat unhealthy foods even occasionally, and I didn't want to see them develop a taste for them. Second, I wanted everybody (especially my children) to get used to the fact that we don't always do or eat as everyone else does. Third, I believe in integrity and in standing by your beliefs.

I know it is hard sometimes. I remember one time when my parents came to visit. My daughter was 14 months old at the time. My father brought some milk chocolate and he insisted on trying to give her a piece despite hearing that she was allergic to both milk and sugar. I didn't agree. And then he said: "I cannot understand why you would deprive your child of such a pleasure." I answered that I believe my child's health to be much more important than her momentary pleasure and that I hoped he would understand someday. Obviously, this wasn't a pleasant conversation. And it wasn't the only one. But with time, my family members and friends realized I was uncompromising in my decision and they gradually stopped looking for opportunities to undermine it.

Apart from the social pressure, transitioning your toddler to veganism should be easy. At this age, kids usually like to try new foods and they still have not developed firm food preferences. So you only have to provide them with lots of healthy plant-based choices.

Young kid

Your kid is growing – he or she is no longer a baby or a toddler who can't voice their opinions – and their social life and social circles are growing too. Your young child goes to a kindergarten or an elementary school, makes new friends, and receives invitations to other kids' parties or even sleepovers. And of course, this opens a whole new arena of challenges for you as a vegan kid's parent.

First of all, you're no longer the only one in charge of your child's menu. Since your child is eating at the kindergarten or at school, you want to make sure she or he keeps eating plant-based and healthy out there. Sometimes this can be challenging. And it all depends on the situation you are in. Some questions you can ask yourself are:

1. Are there any preschools/elementary schools in my area providing a plant-based menu?
2. Can I afford them?

If the answer is yes – great! Case solved. If not, you can ask further:

3. Are there any preschools/elementary schools in my area that would accept my

child's plant-based diet because of health, religious or ethical reasons?

If not, you can ask even further:

4. Are there any preschools/elementary schools in my area that would accept my child bringing his or her own meals to school?

I remember it was very difficult back in Warsaw, Poland, in the 1990s. No public school would provide even a vegetarian diet then. My daughter started her education in 1996 in a private Steiner preschool when she was three. The kindergarten was very expensive, far from our place, the hours were short, and the kids had to bring their own food. Then, when she was four, I started to look for a place closer to our home where she could spend more time. We were very lucky, since there was a nearby public kindergarten for allergic kids. The great thing was, they had their own kitchen with plenty of specialized staff preparing individual diets for kids suffering from all kinds of allergies. She got in because her doctor's certificate said she was allergic to milk and its derivatives, and to sugar. Once she was admitted, I had a meeting with a headmaster. I told her my daughter can't eat any kind of meat as well. The headmaster asked me: "But maybe she could eat some poultry or at least some fish?" My answer was a firm: "No, she cannot have it." The schoolmaster seemed quite shocked and she asked me why. And then I came up with a reason I believed would make sense for her: "For religious reasons." Obviously, it wasn't true, but she was sold. And this way I assured an ovo-vegetarian and no sugar school diet for my daughter.

When my sons reached schooling age — three years old — it was 2010 and we were living in a small Spanish village close to Barcelona called Terrassa. I was friends with a teacher at local school, who told me that the local public schools not only did not provide menus on demand, but moreover they did not accept them even for religious reasons. (They would, for example, feed pork to Muslim kids.)

I could not afford private schooling for two kids at this time. I also wanted to live closer to the Mediterranean Sea, so I started to look for a new apartment and a kindergarten in Barcelona. The headmaster of the first one that had two free places for my twins turned out to be very understanding. I told her my sons were vegan and that I wanted to keep it this way. She asked me why, and I said that it was for ethical reasons. And she said: "No problem." The meals were provided by an external catering company cooperating with several schools in the Barcelona area and were adjusted to each student's individual needs. After several years, I learned that my sons were the only two vegan clients they ever had.

Apart from school menus, there are also the kids' parties and the sleepovers that every parent has to deal with in their own manner. I have developed a special "party policy." Since it seemed quite complicated to ensure my kids would have a plant-based menu at their friends' birthday parties, I used to tell them: "When you're at the party, you can eat whatever you want." And it worked fine for all my kids. As they were old enough to understand our reasons for being vegan, they would never eat meat on purpose, and they asked what was on sandwiches or in a salad. But sometimes they would eat a non-vegan cake without knowing it. As they grew older, they realized that a cake can contain non-vegan products. They asked more and more questions and made more informed choices. Around the age of seven, they started to read the lists of ingredients when shopping or to ask about them when eating out. Nowadays if there's a party with just sandwiches and snacks, they bring their own. If it's a sleepover, I talk to their friends' parents beforehand and bring plant-based burgers or sausages for supper and a plant milk for breakfast. During co-hosted events, I'm always the one responsible for fruits (vegan stereotype) and then each of my sons brings his own vegan cake.

However, sometimes I get really annoyed – for example, when there is a meal to celebrate a school football game and the other parents say, "Where should we go? McDonalds or Burger King?" – as if these were the only and obvious choices. But since my sons are growing bigger and more conscious, I know they can go to either place and order food that may not be healthy but is still vegan.

Teenager

Sometimes kids who weren't raised vegan decide to become vegan, and they often influence other family members. If this is your case, congratulations on raising a compassionate human! If your child was born or raised vegan, then she or he has probably already developed a strong case for being vegan. Kids of this age have a strong sense of morality and individuality, which means they will probably stay vegan despite the fact that outside influences become more important to them than family norms. And even if they experiment with their diet outside of the household, I would not make a big fuss out of it. Being vegan is already a part of their personality. With a bit of luck, they will incorporate veganism as a part of their image inside their peer group.

Let me make a digression to illustrate. My daughter is 27 and my twin sons are 12. All three of them are proud vegans. They announce it and even preach it to everybody willing to listen to them. My daughter convinced her meat-eating fiancé to become vegan. They adopted two cats and they are learning more and more about plant-based cuisine. She makes sure all my cosmetics are vegan and cruelty-free. Both my sons read food ingredient lists and other labels to make sure that whatever we buy is vegan. We have also adopted a cat; both of my sons take care of it and are very sensitive to animals' suffering.

However, changing your kid's diet at this age can be very challenging. If your teenage child wasn't born or raised vegan, it is probable that he or she will not accept the diet change easily or at all. Still, you have much more room to maneuver than with a smaller kid – not only can you prepare tasty and nice-looking plant-based dishes (including veganized versions of their favorite foods), but you can also discuss the health, ethical, and environmental benefits of veganism with them. If you believe they are old enough to face the brutal truth, you can also show them some documentaries on factory farming. But be careful not to over-preach. I met a mother of a teenage daughter recently. She divorced the daughter's father a few years ago and they share custody. The mother met a new partner, and they have become vegan together. The mother would say to me: "I cannot understand my daughter. I keep sending her vegan memes every day, even when she is not staying with me. But she still refuses to go vegan." My only advice to her was to stop pushing her daughter to go vegan.

I transitioned to veganism when my daughter was a teenager, but since she was already vegetarian and did not consume a lot of animal products, I adopted a laid-back attitude. My daughter was vegetarian since birth, but since she was lactose-intolerant, the only animal-based foods she ate until she was eight years old were eggs and butter. When she was eight, her allergy symptoms ceased, so she started consuming some cheese and yogurt. I transitioned to veganism when she was 11. I told her that the dairy and egg industry were very cruel, and that veganism was much better for our health than vegetarianism. This was a difficult time for her, not only because she was starting puberty, but above all because her father and I were divorcing. She didn't really want to listen to my reasons, and I didn't want to come up with any graphic explanations, so I told her it was up to her. I would still buy some eggs, butter, and cheese and keep them in our fridge, but if she wanted to eat them, she had to prepare them herself. And she did. When she was 16, she moved to live with her by-then omnivorous father, who not only respected her choices, but also cooked vegetarian for her. Whenever she stayed with me, she ate plant-based food. When she was 23 and already living on her own, she went vegan without any further prompting from me (apart from my vegan example). She even convinced her omnivorous fiancé to go vegan. Nowadays she says her only regret is not becoming vegan earlier.

We all know the saying that one image is worth a thousand words. But when it comes to parenting, I would paraphrase it to say that one action is worth a thousand words. Our own integrity and example influence and shape our children's minds and behaviors in an incomparably stronger way than our lectures. This becomes especially true and can be seen when our children reach this critical age and start pointing out discrepancies between what we do and what we preach.

So my advice for parents of teenagers is to explain your reasons for going vegan to your kids, but do not expect to sell them on it easily. Just keep providing a good example each day, and hopefully they will come around soon. Remember, how long did it take *you* to become vegan?

3   Challenges

Social pressure

If you already know that veganism is the only truly healthy choice, of course you would like to raise your kid vegan. But it is not always easy because of societal pressure. Some people — your family, friends, acquaintances and even health professionals — will voice their concerns about your child's veganism. Their reactions can sometimes be extreme. But from my own experience I can assure you, the firmer stand you take on your child's veganism, the shorter and smoother these discussions will get.

I remember being a very young and unexperienced mother in 1993. Back then, my family, friends and pediatricians examining my daughter gave me a very hard time. In the best case, they treated my decision to raise her meat and milk-free as a whim, but some of them openly accused me of harming my child. From today's perspective I can say that these opinions hurt me, because deep down I wasn't one hundred percent sure if I was right either. What truly helped me was a lecture I went to when my daughter was two years old. It was given by a brilliant Polish pediatrician, Dr Ewa Pietkiewicz-Rok, who has been recommending vegetarian and vegan diets for children for many years. I remember her saying something like: "Dear parents, when you decide your child will not eat animal products, you are usually concerned about providing all the necessary nutrients. But let's look at it the other way around – once you take this decision – you don't feed your child saturated fats, hormones, antibiotics and other harmful chemicals." For me it was a real eye-opener and a paradigm shift. And of course since then my reactions to the negative comments about my child's diet shifted completely. My only regret was that I didn't come across this argument sooner.

While raising all three of my kids, I heard lots of concerns and unwanted advice from my friends, from family members, and even from complete strangers after they learned that my kids did not eat a standard diet. My sons are 12 now, and I still hear these concerns from time to time. Let me give you a recent example. My sons started junior high in 2019. I had meetings with some of their new teachers. One of them asked me about our veganism and I explained that I am a vegan health coach. And five minutes later the same teacher asked me, if my son's cold and five-day absence in December was not caused by his vegan diet. I had to make a big effort to change my laugh to smile and assure her, that my sons are the healthiest eating children, that I know. I also made a point about them being twins and obviously eating the same diet. (Let's face it children get cold sometimes, even the vegan coach's ones). As you can see nowadays, I can treat such situation as an anecdote, because I've come such a long way since I've decided not to feed dead animals' bodies to my children. These days not only I am not annoyed by such situations, I am on the contrary happy, since they provide me with a great excuse to smile and preach veganism.

People will use all sorts of arguments to undermine your decision – from health-related to even religious. The four most common arguments people make against raising children vegan are:

1. "Your baby/child won't grow and/or be healthy without consuming animal products." Lots of health professionals nowadays admit that a plant-based diet is healthy for adults, but still they don't believe it's appropriate for babies and

small children. Some years before, they would have said the same about vegetarianism. Luckily, the times are changing. Since it is a well-established fact that the plant-based diet contains all the necessary nutrients, why would you feed your child something else? Would you want to add harmful substances to her diet? Don't get into the debate on proteins – there's plenty of protein in plant-based foods. And if there are any protein-related problems in a modern society, it's the excessive intake of animal protein, which is the root of many "civilization diseases," such as cancer, diabetes and obesity. Don't get into a debate on cow's milk either – cow's milk is a perfect food for baby calves, who develop a large body mass and a little brain mass rapidly. A perfect food for a human baby is a human milk. If you can't breastfeed for some reason, there are some plant-based baby formulas. And once your child starts to eat other foods, even these are unnecessary.

2. "You're not giving your child a choice." It's so absurd, it really astonishes me

each time I hear this one. As if raising your child an omnivore meant giving them a choice. Being a parent means making choices for your child. You choose not only what to feed him, but also how to dress him, what diapers to use, and how to play with him. Babies and small children cannot choose for themselves. It's a parent's duty and responsibility to make choices for them. So of course it's your choice what to feed your kids. And if we know that veganism is the healthiest diet, we will choose it for our children. At some point your kid will develop her own taste preferences, but still it doesn't mean you should let her eat whatever she wants. Let's say your kid likes sweets. Since sweets are not the healthiest choice, even plant-based ones, you wouldn't let your kid eat only vegan sweets. It's your responsibility to keep your child's diet healthy.

3. "You'll see — when your kids get older, they will go to McDonalds and love it" or "your children will be social misfits." I used to reply: "We'll see." And I'm proud to announce neither is the case.

Moreover, all my kids have been to McDonalds at some point – eating only vegan stuff of course, but they are not huge fans. All of them like (vegan) burgers and hot dogs, but they prefer to eat them in vegan establishments, where they have a genuine choice. And all three of them are proud vegans who advocate for both animal and human rights. They are popular at school and in their social circles. And I dare to say some part of this is due to their off-beat and uncompromising attitude. For example, when my sons were 10, I met a mother of a friend of theirs, who told me there was a workshop on ecology at their school. And afterwards her son told her: "Mom, I believe we should be more ecology-oriented. Look at Olaf and Igor – we should be more like them."

4. "If someday by chance your children eat some animal products, they will get really sick." Nothing like this has happened. My daughter used to have a very intense social life in the kindergarten. She and her friends would run around the housing development in the afternoon playing outside and

visiting one another. And of course, at mealtime the parents would offer their kids and the visiting kids something to eat. My daughter would always ask what they were having in order to judge if it was vegetarian or not. I remember one day she came back from her friend's house after dinner. I asked her what she had there, and she replied "a broth." I didn't want her to be upset or to cause any kind of psychosomatic reaction, so I just asked her if she liked it and she said no. I waited until the next day to explain to her that what we call "a broth" at home is vegan, whereas for most people it means "a chicken or a meat broth." But she felt perfectly fine.

Usually, it's the interactions between vegan parents and non-vegan grandparents (and other close family members) that are the most difficult to manage. When you decide to raise your child vegan, it can sometimes turn the family gatherings into a battlefield. The more you are connected to your family and the more they are opposed to veganism, the harder and more painful these situations become. Especially since you want to visit your family and you want them to get to know your child, but the last thing you want your kid to see are fights over his or her meals.

The main difficulty in this scenario is that when you are an inexperienced parent, lots of people (especially close relatives or friends who already have kids) feel entitled to give you their advice. My recommendation is that once you have announced that your baby will be vegan, if the reaction wasn't positive, do not encourage them to advise you. Avoid asking them any diet-related questions. Of course, you can still ask them a hundred questions about what they did or would do about sleeping, breastfeeding, baby clothes, toys and other subjects. But from my experience, I can tell you that these conversations can sometimes take strange turns and come back to food again. If they still preach, do not engage in a discussion, just say something like "thank you—I appreciate your concern, but I know what I'm doing." Even if that reply is very often not 100 percent true (especially with the first child), I believe your doubts about your kid's plant-based diet can be much better addressed by people who have expertise in raising children this way (the same goes for many other topics). I remember my mother couldn't help me when I was breastfeeding my daughter, since she hadn't breastfed me and my siblings. On the contrary, her concerns voiced in good faith only confused me. She needed to see me breastfeeding my kids and raising them vegan to believe it was an optimal solution. Nowadays she is a big advocate of both.

If your dear ones ask for the reasons behind your decision, I would stick strictly to the baby's health (I wouldn't go into discussing the tradition, animal welfare, or environmental issues). Of course, sometimes people will try to undermine your arguments about veganism being the healthiest option to raise your child, so you might want to prepare your talking points beforehand.

As I said before, I fought a real battle with my family once – over 27 years ago, when my first child was born. And believe me, it was very hard, especially since I was a very young mother (only 23 years old), and I felt like I needed a lot of help and support. But on the other hand, it was my daughter who made me question the standard Western diet and look for a better alternative in the first place. When I was pregnant, a lot of my childhood memories came back to me. As I mentioned above, one of the most vivid realizations was that meat is a dead animal's flesh. I could clearly remember the shock, disgust and sadness I felt when my parents answered my question about where meat comes from. And at that very moment I promised myself that I was not going to do that to my own child.

I was sure I did not want my child to eat meat, poultry, and fish, and since my family members were strongly opposed to this idea, I turned elsewhere for advice, finding vegan-friendly private pediatricians and support groups that helped me a lot at the beginning.

What also really helped at this time was being about to cite the newest findings, clinical test results and literature. I also pointed out the obvious mistakes in my diet as a child – for example being forced to consume cow's milk, despite being allergic to it. I've done so not to blame my parents, but to open their eyes to how the animal-food industry propaganda works and to the fact that nutrition is evolving as a science.

Later, when I didn't crave anyone's approval for my decision, and everybody could see my daughter growing – slim but healthy, both physically and intellectually – I even influenced my family of origin to become vegetarian. And I am very proud to say my mother still is one at the age of 72.

Making the transition

If you are reading this, you are probably thinking about transitioning your child's diet (and maybe your own diet, too) to veganism, or you are in the process of doing so.

I strongly believe this can be done at any stage of a kid's life and it can only be beneficial. Like many other kinds of changes, you can take it slowly or decide to do it all at once.

I would consider the former course – changing gradually – only during pregnancy, or if you were consuming lots of animal products and highly-processed foods. If this is your situation, I probably wouldn't go cold turkey, since your body's detoxification process could be a bit unpleasant (possible headaches, bowel disruption, fatigue or anxiety, for example). However, if you are vegetarian or if your diet was relatively healthy until now – containing lots of vegetables, whole grains, legumes and fruits and few animal products, I don't see any reason for you not to make the complete change at the very moment you make up your mind.

Transitioning while pregnant or having a small baby should be easy – it's just a question of changing your dietary habits. Making the transition at any other stage of your child's life may seem difficult mainly for psychological reasons. I mean, if your kid is already used to some animal products (or highly-processed foods, which you should cut out, too), they may crave them and show or voice their complaints. The key here is your own integrity. If you have made up your mind to provide your kid with healthy plant-based nutrition, just stick to it. You know that it's in your child's best interest to become vegan, and the sooner the better. Remember that lots of animal products and highly-processed foods are addictive to some extent. Therefore, you have to be firm about your decision. If your child is asking for animal products, remember he or she does not need them — on the contrary, these foods are harmful. Your child could have developed a craving for these unhealthy foods — not only for animal products, but also for sweets and sodas — and now he doesn't understand why he cannot have them anymore.

Your child will accept the change much more easily if she sees that you are also involved. I strongly believe in being a role model versus preaching or forbidding. I would not go into a lengthy explanation about my decision to toddlers or young children, but I would try to make the transition seamless or at least easy for them instead. For example, if your kid loves burgers or pasta, I would serve them plant-based burgers and pasta. The same goes for ice cream, cakes, and cheese. Nowadays you can buy or prepare a vegan version of any food or dish. You don't want your child to think that veganism means sacrificing all of their favorite foods.

If your child notices the changes in the menu, and asks about them, you can provide an explanation appropriate for his or her age. You don't even have to mention the word "vegan" to a toddler. You can just say something like: "I've learned about these new foods, and I thought we could try them." If your child keeps asking questions, they are probably ready for a more thorough explanation. In that case you can try touching on the health subject – for example: "I've heard that people who eat these foods are healthier and stronger. And the kids who eat them grow healthier. You want to be strong and healthy, don't you?" When you believe it is in your kid's best interest, you just do whatever it takes to put him on the healthy plant-based track. However, if your child is older or keeps investigating the subject, you can mention animal welfare at some point. It all depends on your kid's maturity and sensibility. I wouldn't go into any graphic descriptions of the evils of animal farming, but I would stress that your new vegan lifestyle promotes animal well-being. (Older kids usually respond much better to the ethical arguments than to the health-related ones.)

It is worth considering that children may make the transition easily, because their perception is still "fresh" — innocent and free of the cultural categories and norms we live by without even noticing them. I'll offer two stories that illustrate this point.

My friend's son had a cuddly toy chicken, and one day, when his mother called him for dinner saying, "We are going to have chicken tonight," the boy became terrified (he was four at the time). He asked, "The chicken – like my chicken toy?" And his mother explained, "No, not at all. There are chickens and grocery chickens. They are completely different species." I have no idea how long she got away with this lie. But certainly, by the time the boy realized it was a monstrous lie, his meat-eating habits and taste were much better established.

Another story also illustrates the more innocent or natural ethics of children. A group of city children around 10 years old went for a camp in the countryside. They stayed at an organic farm with lots of animals. On the first afternoon they visited the farm and the owners encouraged them to play with and feed the animals – a calf among others. The kids enjoyed the activity and liked the animals. The next evening a dinner was served. And when the kids asked what dish it was, the answer was: "veal." The children made the connection quickly – they refused to eat it and were very sad.

The most difficult phase for your child's transition to veganism is adolescence. But anything is just more difficult with teenagers, isn't it? If your kid is already in a rebel phase, he or she will probably also confront you about the diet change. If this is the case, there are three ways to go about it: hands on, hands off, and something in between. The upside of dealing with your teenager's complaints is that you can provide her or him with thorough information (even the graphic stuff) to support your decision. The downside is that your teenager will probably be eager to question or reject it. Keep in mind that a lot depends on how you present your arguments. Remember the story I told in the previous chapter about the mother of the teenager who kept sending her daughter vegan memes? She didn't convince her daughter, and probably just annoyed her.

But since veganism is getting more and more popular, you may end up surprised at how easily your teenagers gets on board with your new lifestyle. And if it is your experience – congratulations! If not, you will have some hard choices to make. Remember, you are the parent and you are setting the boundaries. The completely hands-off attitude consists of providing your kid with the same old diet and just providing a vegan example, whereas the completely hands-on attitude can be summed up as something like "my house, my rules." And of course, there are many more ways of making the transition in between the hands-on and hands-off approaches. You can say to your teenager: "You can eat anything you want outside of the house, but I'm not going to buy, have or cook any animal products here." Or you can say: "I'm going to cook vegan meals from now on. If you want to eat something else at home, you will need to prepare it yourself." In any case I wouldn't go to war over veganism. I heard about a case when parents of teenage kid became vegan and tried to force it on him by bombarding the kid with graphic information on a factory farming cruelty. The result was quite the opposite of the one they expected and hoped for.

I had this kind of experience myself when I was transitioning from vegetarianism to veganism, as I've described above, when my daughter was 11 years old. My task was fairly easy, since she was vegetarian from birth and the only animal products she ate were eggs, cheese, yogurt, and butter. I told her I was going to be vegan and explained why. She wasn't on board at the time, so I told her I would keep buying her these animal products, if she wanted, but I would not prepare them for her. Neither of us was very happy at the time, but we both put up with this decision. She would make herself scrambled eggs or cheese sandwiches from time to time, but most of the time she would just eat the plant-based meals that I cooked. (Did I mention that many teenagers tend to be lazy? It worked really well for my daughter.) She stayed vegetarian for a few more years, even when she wasn't living in vegetarian households. And when she was 23, she proudly announced that she had become vegan, and then she influenced her fiancé to transition to veganism.

Non-vegan co-parent

If you are new to the vegan lifestyle and your partner doesn't seem to be interested in it, you can feel a little lost and lonesome. If this is your case, I really hope this chapter will help you. However, if you have been vegan for some time already, you and your non-vegan partner have probably developed a modus operandi that works for both of you. But even in a best-case-scenario, when a new member of the family comes to this world, things tend to get more complicated, and I am not talking only about the diet. Usually it is not only the parents who are involved. When you expect a child – especially the first one – the grandparents and other more experienced family members feel qualified to give you plenty of advice. And this pressure starts as early as they learn about the pregnancy. In cases when one of the parents decides to shift to veganism later and wants to change their kid's diet as well, the reactions can be similar.

If you are raising a child together with your non-vegan partner, reaching an agreement on how you will do it is vital. And obviously your child's diet is a very important part of it. There are many scenarios possible depending on your relationship, culture, etc. The most absurd one

I heard about, was of a couple, who planned to have kids (she was a vegan and he was an omnivore) and they decided that if they have a girl, she would be vegan, whereas if they have a boy, he would eat a standard Western diet.

I believe that the most important consideration in a discussion between a vegan and a non-vegan parent or future parents should be your child's health. It is my personal view that all other factors like tradition, religion, etc. are far less important. If you are reading this chapter, you are probably the vegan parent and you want to raise your kid this way. So to get the non-vegan co-parent on board with your decision, you should persuade them that veganism is the best for your child's health. But here it gets tricky. If your partner believes it, why wouldn't they choose it themselves? It doesn't really make sense, but I have met many couples with kids in which one parent cooks and eats vegan together with their child, whereas the other keeps eating animal products despite knowing that veganism is the best diet.

I can say from observation that even though we live in the twenty-first century, it is mostly women who make the dietary decisions in their households, mainly because they are usually still the ones doing the cooking. And when I come across a heterosexual couple who are vegan and non-vegan, the vast majority of the vegans are women. (This is probably a topic for a whole new book, but I believe that a reason the female-male ratio in the vegan population is so unequal has its deep cultural roots in a "real male" or a "hunter" stereotype.) All in all, I hear about lots of couples with children where the mother and a child or children are vegan, but the father, even if he is on board with this decision, occasionally eats some animal products. If this is your case, I believe setting some ground rules is vital. I mean, if your partner wants to eat some non-vegan products, you should agree on several things beforehand. Will he eat them in front of your child? Will he buy them when you are shopping together? Will he cook and consume them at home? What will you tell your kids, when they find it out?

As I said, your non-vegan partner may be perfectly happy that your child will be vegan. However, if it is not the case, you may want to prepare yourself for a discussion by doing some research and finding data to support your decision beforehand. Stick to the arguments about your child's health, and do not get into a discussion about choice or a lack of it. Of course, raising your child vegan is a decision and you can prove it is beneficial for their health. Feeding your child a standard Western diet is another decision, and you can prove it can harm your child's health. Also prepare for the standard questions vegans get asked all the time about protein, calcium, iron, vitamin B-12 and D. (Even if your partner won't ask them, you will hear them elsewhere.)

Poor eater

My relationship with food wasn't always as and happy as it is nowadays. As a child I was labeled a poor eater. I remember my parents' constant worry about my weight, my health, and my not eating. My ambition as a mother was to avoid all this with my kids, and I can proudly announce I've succeeded. All my kids are and have always been great eaters – they like to eat, and they are always curious and eager to discover new dishes, cuisines and foods. When people hear that my children like to eat virtually all kinds of vegetables and whole grains, they say, "lucky you!" But luck has nothing to do with it – I achieved it by applying the policies I discuss in this chapter.

Be an example

Many parents complain that their children don't like "veggies" or "greens" or other healthy foods. They say things like "my 11-year-old son doesn't eat any vegetables." Or "I don't think she has ever had broccoli in her life." On such occasions I feel like asking, "Do *you* enjoy eating vegetables?" Or "Do *you* eat broccoli?" Setting a good example cannot be overestimated.

In my opinion, your beliefs (including the hidden ones) are crucial. Are you positive that unprocessed vegan foods are the best for your child and that your child won't be deprived or miss out on anything eating that way? I would like to propose a thought experiment that will help you evaluate your attitude towards food. Please think about the snacks or foods that first come to mind that you would serve your child in the following situations:

a) Your children are sad – they have lost their favorite toy, had a fight with their best friend or didn't pass an exam.

b) Your children are happy – it's their birthday or they have won a competition.

c) Your children are sick, but they tell you they're hungry.

Those situations in which we ourselves resort to either comfort or celebratory foods, best show our deepest beliefs. If it turns out that you are more or less consciously concerned that your kid will miss out on things because of being vegan, I would like to encourage you to work on shifting your paradigm. If you don't do it, you will pass your doubts on to your child, who will probably feel them and make use of them. This is especially important, since our food habits, starting with comfort foods, are shaped in the course of our childhood and can affect the rest of our lives. (Let me ask you another question here: what are *your* comfort foods?)

To summarize: if you eat only a variety of healthy foods and this is what you serve in your household, your child is left with no choice but a healthy one.

Don't label or compare

I often hear parents complaining about their kids' eating habits. They label them "poor eaters" or "picky." Hence another policy of mine — not using labels. Since labels stick, I believe labeling doesn't help. And the same goes for comparing. The sooner you accept your child's individuality and stop comparing them with others, the better for everyone. Let me give you a personal example. When my nonidentical twin sons were born, the first one weighed 2980 g (6.57 lbs) and measured 50 cm (19.69 inches), and the second one, 2890 g (6.37 lbs) and 51 cm (20.1 inches). They were so similar that everybody thought they were identical twins and had problems telling them apart. Obviously, they had the same diet. But over time, my second son grew much faster. Both are now 12, and my second son is so much taller than his twin brother that people ask me what the age difference is between them. But since they're both healthy and happy, I don't worry.

I advise parents to worry less and to try to think about their children in a positive way. For example, if your kid is not a big eater, but is healthy and radiant, say: "My daughter may not eat a lot, but she gets all her body needs." If your son is not enthusiastic about many of dishes you serve him, you can say: "He's still discovering and looking for his favorite foods."

Don't worry

Some parents worry about their child's appetite so much that they start to count how much he or she eats. My secret to raising a good eater is to always remember that healthy children do not starve themselves. That is why I am never worried if my children do not eat or eat very little – it happens very rarely, since usually they eat a lot and ask for more, but if they do not feel well or lose their appetite for some reason, I never panic and I let them leave their plate full or half full. It almost always happens when they have a fever, but sometimes it happens even before any other symptoms of an infection are present. And I do not try to persuade them to eat anything if they say they are not hungry. I believe their body knows what it is doing, directing all its energy to address the sickness, instead of using it to digest foods. I only make sure they drink plenty of water.

Babies and toddlers can lose their appetite due to teething and sometimes they just get too tired to eat, especially if their daily schedule or physical activity is changing – such as when they give up their daily nap or they start to crawl or walk, or if they're getting through an especially hot day. So if your kid gets whiny and refuses to eat, it can be better to put them down for a nap or soothe them first, and then feed them.

Other reason for not eating – especially in a case of older children and teenagers – can be stress. Sometimes they need to talk about their problems and get them out of their system first. But not all children will readily talk about their problems. If you see your child is stressed out, you can take them for a walk, play sports or a board game with them, or watch a movie together – just to help them refocus their attention and take their mind off their problem (if only just for a while). Afterwards, they may regain their composure and (especially after a physical activity) also their appetite.

Give them time

I believe problems arise when parents are afraid that their child doesn't eat enough, and they start to literally chase a kid with a spoon throughout the house or even on the playground. Or they switch on a TV and feed their kid in front of it, which turns eating into a mechanical and imposed action, instead of a joyful feast.

I often see worried parents trying to feed their children some snacks or asking if they are hungry every couple of hours. A child who has a bite here and there can never get really hungry, and therefore will never feel like eating a big meal. I believe babies and small toddlers can eat five meals a day. But as they grow, I would try to reduce it to three solid meals and two smaller snacks. But I wouldn't provide a poor eater with any other snacks – nothing but water and fresh fruits and veggies in between meals (with the exception of bananas and avocados – they're so satiating that I would rather incorporate them into a main meal). I would also be even more conscious about her or his diet, if your kid eats very little. The less space there is in her or his tummy, the more reason to fill every inch of it with only the highest quality, nutrient-rich foods. And obviously there's no place for any junk food — even vegan junk foods.

So if your kid is refusing to eat, my advice is not to panic. Just let them wait until they are hungry. After all, you don't want food to become the focus of power plays between you and your child, right? My experience tells me that after skipping a meal or eating very little for a day or two, healthy kids always go back to eating and enjoying it.

Set limits

If your kid refused to eat a particular dish, you can propose that they eat more of other dishes instead. Let's say, for example, you have soup as a first course, and rice with vegetables as a second. If the soup is not your kid's favorite, you can agree they will just eat a bigger plate of the second course. Just make sure your kid eats a healthy vegan meal. Of course, I know it gets more complicated when there's more than one kid, since I have been single-handedly raising my twin sons for years. When each one of them is asking for a different dish and saying he hates his brother's choice, I just tell them our home is not a restaurant and that we do not have a menu from which to choose. Moreover, I remind them that I also have my top ten plates, which may not be their favorites. So we agree we will each take turns eating somebody's favorite dish. (Sometimes we even flip a coin to establish the order.)

But this is not the case with desserts, of course. I believe that desserts are optional. Even healthy ones usually provide fewer nutrients and fiber than a regular meal. So I don't consider them a regular meal substitute and I do not want them to become one.

If my kids want to eat a dessert, they have to eat the main course first. In fact, if I want to make sure that one of my children is not just being picky about a particular food, but is genuinely not interested in eating at the moment, because they do not feel well, I sometimes run a little test. I say they can get one of their favorite desserts if they finish the main course first. If they show an interest in the dessert, I assume that they are just being picky. Whereas if they do not feel well, they just say they're not hungry no matter what.

Give choices

Giving your child a choice and a vote on what to eat is very important. I'm not talking about absolute freedom of choice, I'm talking about a choice between two or more healthy alternatives. You can simply ask them what they'd like when planning your menu or writing your shopping list. But it's often easier just to give them an option to choose between two or more healthy alternatives. Another way is to prepare a dish that can be personalized. Let me give you some examples:

Homemade pizza: you prepare or buy whole meal pizza crusts and then you give everyone a choice of sauce: tomato, plant-based cheese or olive oil with herbs; and then for the toppings, the sky is the limit: peppers, onions, olives, tomatoes, mushrooms, corn, etc. Everybody can come up with their favorite ingredients.

Burritos/tacos/crepes: you provide a whole grain base and then fill it with beans, vegan cheese, onions, lettuce, tomatoes, spinach, corn, etc. And again, everybody can come up with their favorite fillings.

Dips: prepare a number of plant-based dips and creams, hummus, guacamole, tomato sauce, plant-based cheese dip, etc. and then serve them with raw vegetables such as carrots, cucumbers, peppers, celery, etc., or eat them with vegan breadsticks or chips.

Engage them

Engaging your kids can really work miracles. If you can get your kids involved in food planning and preparation, they will be much more likely to enjoy the final result. You can start by involving them in choosing the menu, and then you can go together shopping for the ingredients. And sometimes it can be the other way around — you go shopping with your kids, and they can find some new foods or ones you know but forgot about. I would say go for these new foods if you want to engage your children in your diet, and then incorporate these freshly (re)discovered foods into your menu.

Your kids can help you in the kitchen, too – the little ones can be satisfied and proud to choose the salad ingredients and then to mix them all together. They can also mix the batter ingredients. I remember how proud my sons were at the ages of three and four when we used to prepare bread dough and then bake the bread together. Older kids can go in for more ambitious recipes. They can wash, peel, grate or even cut the vegetables – depending on their age, manual skills, and preferences. The dishes with a choice of ingredients, such as those I talked about above (pizza, tacos, etc.) can also be a way of engaging your kid in food preparing – especially the ones who do not want to shop or cook together. Funnily enough, I've seen children whose parents labelled them as "poor eaters," after co-preparing a meal of their choice, not only eat it up, but also ask for more.

Offer variety

There are thousands of edible vegetables, grains and fruits in the world and there are almost unlimited ways to prepare them, so I believe everybody can find recipes they would like. But your child may have to try many dishes in order to discover the ones he or she likes. So variety and experimentation are key. And besides that, trying new foods is the opposite of boredom and routine. At the end of the day, I believe that eating should be an interesting and joyful experience.

I can already hear parents who say, "But my kid will only eat...." And I believe that that is sometimes the case. But if your child didn't learn to eat a variety of foods and to enjoy trying new ones at an earlier stage of life, this can always change. And I would say it should – not only because it is easier to live with a kid who eats a wide variety of foods, but also because it is simply healthier; a repetitive diet, even one consisting of the healthiest ingredients, can lead to nutritional deficiencies.

Surprisingly enough, sometimes the kids who would not touch particular foods or try the new ones at home are willing to try them somewhere else. If this is the case with your child, I advise you to take your kid out at the nearest possibility and encourage them to try the new foods somewhere else. It can be your friends' house, a restaurant, or a trip to a place where people eat differently — and where your kid's regular food is "not available." Even if that's not entirely true, you can use a change of scene to open your child to new tastes. And when you're back home, you can evoke those pleasant memories by cooking and eating those new menu items yourselves.

My house can be the best example of such a place. As I've said before, my sons are the only vegans at their school. Whenever they have visitors, whether just for an afternoon or a whole sleepover, I serve everybody our usual plant-based dishes. And then, when I tell my sons' friends' parents what their children had eaten (and enjoyed), they can't believe it. Very recently, for example, a girl stayed at our house for dinner and I told her mother she had eaten beetroot soup. The mother said: "What? Beetroot soup? How do you even make that?" I laughed and told her that her daughter was very enthusiastic about it, since she saw one in a game she plays with my son – Minecraft – and that she liked it very much. Another of my sons' friends kept asking her mum, "Can we please have these tasty little white balls that we have for breakfast at Joanna's place?" At first, I couldn't put my finger on it. But then it occurred to me that she was referring to millet, which I often serve for breakfast with apple sauce. I don't know if it is due to our "vegan house magic" or something else, but I've noticed that during recent sleepovers, each of four kids ate half a kilogram (about one pound) of grapes for dessert.

Travelling

While travelling with your kids should be a wonderful experience that fulfills what you've all been anticipating and dreaming about, it can turn out to be a quite a nightmare sometimes. If you've ever travelled with a hungry toddler or a grumpy teenager, you know what I mean.

There are two stages to a trip. The first one is the travelling itself – I mean getting from your home to another destination via whatever form of transportation, and then returning home. The other phase is being there – when you spend some time in a new place.

Try to have an easygoing attitude about both stages. I would of course keep it vegan, but I would be more flexible and open-minded about plant-based nutrition standards than I tend to be in my everyday life. I mean, I would not expect my family to have the same high-quality, whole, plant-based foods as they usually do at home. Believe me, your kids will welcome the change – after all, trying new things is what a journey is all about, isn't it?

In my experience, the travelling itself tends to be much more complicated diet-wise than staying in a new place. For example, airports can be a vegan desert – they tend to have a very limited choice of foods at very high prices. A few years ago, the airports I went through most frequently (Barcelona, Spain – where I live, and Warsaw, Poland – my hometown) didn't have anything plant-based to offer apart from French fries and salad consisting of lettuce, tomatoes and cucumbers. Nowadays, I see a slight change – there are some vending machines and some snack bars where you can at least buy a hummus and grilled vegetable sandwich.

Anyway, I advise you to prepare for your trip beforehand by making homemade snacks and bringing them with you. Then you'll just have to buy water or fruit juice. What snacks? I opt for homemade sandwiches or wraps (with hummus or guacamole, vegetables and tempeh or tofu), diced fruit, cupcakes, nuts, seeds, power balls or bars, and chips (homemade vegetable chips are the best: carrots, beetroot, kale, parsley, etc.). However, if you can't prepare them beforehand, don't give up! I'm sure you can find something plant-based to eat even in the most vegan-hostile environment. The main problem with fast-food snack bars or stands is that they cannot customize your food. So just look through their menu carefully and pick out the items that might be vegan, and then ask if they truly are. The most common vegan items in a fast-food facility are French fries, salads (green salad, tabbouleh, etc.), garlic bread, onion rings, fruit salad... and that's pretty much it. For the salads, you can ask if they have them readymade or if they mix the ingredients; in the latter case, you can ask for a salad without cheese/shrimp, etc., but be prepared to pay the whole price. You can usually also buy vegan snacks foods like chips, nuts and bread sticks at a stall, but then you have to make sure to buy lots of water, too, since they all tend to be over-salted.

As for staying in another place where you're not cooking yourself, it will differ. In a big town, there should be no problem with finding some vegan or at least vegan-friendly places (one site I recommend for helping find them is https://www.happycow.net/ website or app).

If you're staying in an all-inclusive resort, you should be able to find many plant-based options. However, on some occasions, I could not find enough of them and I talked to the managers and asked them to take my dietary preferences into account. In my experience, these people are very keen on pleasing their customers and they will go the extra mile to make you and your children happy. That's how we got a plant-based milk for breakfast in the Canary Islands, falafel for lunch and dinner (instead of breakfast only) in Egypt, pasta and rice with a vegan sauces in Turkey, and vegan pizza in Italy.

If you're staying in a smaller town with no vegan-friendly places, you'll have to improvise. You can find a nice, small (family-owned) restaurant, explain your preferences to the staff, and see what they can prepare for you. Hopefully, they will be able to veganize (exclude or replace some ingredients) some of their dishes. However, if they don't understand you, try to buy basic starters and garnish, like: steamed vegetables, potatoes, and salads. They may come in small quantities, but they are most likely to be plant-based. And if they turn out to be good, you can just order more of them.

If you can choose from among ethnic cuisines, the ones most likely to have vegan plates will be Mediterranean (Italian, Arabian, Greek) and Asian (Indian, Thai, Chinese, Japanese).

Below is by no means complete list of the most common plant-based dishes from different cuisines (of course recipes can differ – so please check the ingredients before ordering):

- International: French fries, grilled or baked potatoes, onion rings, grilled or steamed vegetables, vegetable salad, green salad, fruit salad, sorbet, carrot cake, baked beans
- Asian: rice or noodles with vegetables (no egg); falafel; hummus, babaganush, moutabal, and other eastern dips; vegetable wok (no egg); vegetable moussaka, vegetable couscous, tabbouleh, pita, halva
- Italian: pizza or focaccia with vegetables (no cheese); pasta with tomato, aglio e olio, Putinesque or Marinara sauce; vegetable or mushroom risotto (no cream or cheese); artichokes a la Romana
- Spanish: pan con tomate pimientos de Padron, paella de verduras, guacamole, gazpacho, salmorejo, ajo blanco, patatas fritas, patatas arrugadas, macedonia (fruit salad), compota de frutas
- Japanese: vegetable sushi, miso soup (no bonito), edamame, vegetable

tempura, vegetable gyoza, wakame salad, tofu, mochi (no milk)

A personal note: I recently stayed in Venice, Italy, with my sons. We were all thrilled to taste real Italian food, but honestly, there was hardly anything plant-based on the menus. (And they didn't serve my favorite dish, artichokes a la Romana – probably since Italy is much bigger than I thought). After several trials of finding a restaurant with plant-based items on the menu, we just entered the first one and did our best to explain what we wanted. It turned out they could prepare a vegetable pizza without cheese, and they had vegan gnocchi or pasta with pesto or tomato sauce and they served a parmesan cheese on the side. They even had some plant-based ice-cream options. It took me a long time to spot a coffee shop where they would serve a plant-milk latte, but it was worth it and I still miss its rich, creamy taste and texture.

So my personal advice is to take it easy, talk to the local people, and enjoy your trip!

How much to tell your child

There is no obvious answer to this question. In an ideal world, you wouldn't have to explain anything to your child, since veganism would simply be a universal standard that nobody would question. I believe this is the future. But meanwhile, it's much more likely that the older your kid grows, the more they will notice differences between your diet and your lifestyle and that of others and will ask for explanations.

The most obvious explanation is that veganism is good for your health. Young children will be happy to hear they're growing strong and healthy eating a vegan diet. Teenagers may find appealing the idea of being slim, fit and having healthy skin (acne is often diet-related). However, I believe that most older kids will be far more interested in not taking part in animal exploitation and in having a positive impact on the environment. Many parents dread discussing with their children mass animal killing, global warming, and hunger in the third world. I can certainly relate to that – these are very difficult topics and we don't want to blight their childhoods or scare them. But on the other hand, I believe that if children are asking for more detailed explanations, it may mean they are ready for them.

How much to tell and when will of course depend on your child's age, individual sensitivity, and intellectual capacity. I believe that kids differ among themselves as much as adults. Some children can live in a Neverland until they are eight years old or even older despite high intellectual abilities, while others start to investigate the world around them in a pretty rational manner already at the age of four.

Since you are the world's biggest expert on your kid, it is your decision and therefore your responsibility to choose what, when and how to tell your child about veganism.

In the case of a small child, your explanations will serve to justify and express your lifestyle in the world around you. But as your kid's social circle and interactions grow, they will be asked more questions (and they will ask more questions themselves). Your arguments will serve as a point of reference and a model that your children will use when faced with outside influences and challenges.

Let me give you an example. When my sons were nine years old (and already eating plant-based school meals for six years), one of them heard a new school canteen monitor say, "I believe that people should eat everything." My son, who voices all his opinions easily when with his friends, found it difficult to face an adult and therefore he said nothing. But that day after school, he told me what happened. Being a vegan in a non-vegan world sometimes is a challenge even for adults, so imagine how it can be for kids. Of course, I contacted the school and let them know that I didn't appreciate this comment. I told them that they should respect both my sons' diet and their lifestyle philosophy, since in our case veganism is not only a diet but also reflects our ethical views. They apologized, and it never happened again.

The older your child grows, the more often her or his veganism will be questioned. When asked for their reasons, they will no longer feel like saying nothing or saying "because my mom says so." They will be expected, and more importantly, they will want, to justify it themselves. And that is why explaining to your kid why being vegan is the best choice is so important. Fortunately there are more and more vegan books and movies for children.

There are a lot of movies you can watch

with your young kid, like "Babe" or "Babe: Pig in the City." And you can tell them that the main actor, James Cromwell, became vegan precisely because of a part he played in them. Then there is also "Chicken Run" and many others.

In the case of teenagers, there's plenty of vegan information available online (e.g. Netflix or YouTube). I wouldn't recommend very graphic materials to anybody who is not an adult. (But on the other hand, I've met a lot of people who became vegans after watching "Earthlings.")

4   Everyday tips

Four tenets

Depending on your child's age and if you're transitioning his or her diet to veganism or if your child is already vegan, my practical tips differ. But four things always stand: integrity, flavor, presentation, and choice.

Integrity

We say that one image is worth a thousand words. So let's say one good example is worth a thousand words. Therefore, if you are vegan and you stress the importance of a healthy diet, make sure you are eating one as well. Make sure you don't buy or keep the foods you don't approve of in your household. Don't make exceptions for your guests – show your kid that veganism is something you believe in, you stand for, and you are proud of. You can make some exceptions when visiting with somebody; I don't mean eating meat, dairy, eggs, or other animal products, just eating less healthy, but still vegan foods, specifically when you know they were prepared especially for you. However, if you are going to a place where there's nothing for you to eat, I would bring my own food. The same goes for restaurants – if there's no vegan choice, I would ask the waiters, if some foods can be veganized – for example: vegetarian pizza with no cheese, or sushi with just vegetables. (My sons order oriental chicken & vegetable noodles without chicken all the time.) This way you show your child (and all the world) your integrity, and how to teach others to respect your lifestyle.

When you are transitioning to veganism, but you are still not sure if you will eat exclusively plant-based from now on, inform them this is what you are doing (of course, if they are still babies or toddlers, there's no need for such an explanation – they probably won't notice the difference). I'm talking about small or bigger children and teenagers – from my own experience I know, the bigger the kid, the more they notice your inconsistency. However, if you're going vegan cold turkey, tell your kid and be absolutely sure and firm about it.

Flavor

The food should taste good – pretty obvious, isn't it? If you're already vegan, you know how to prepare healthy plant-based dishes, which all your family enjoys. However, if you're transitioning, it can be a little tricky, since your kid has already developed her palate and tastes for some non-vegan foods, and you are probably still learning vegan cuisine. In that case, my advice is not to make it a revolution and therefore a big challenge. Take an easy way out. You have already been cooking some plant-based dishes, and also some which take very little to be veganized (for example, ones in which you can use plant oil instead of butter or plant milk instead of cow's). Then you can veganize your kid's favorite dishes. There are two ways to go about veganizing your favorite dishes – either you stick to your regular recipes and just replace non-vegan ingredients with vegan ones, or you look for new, plant-based recipes for your favorite dishes.

Let me share my experience here. My children weren't introduced to many mainstream staple dishes because of their vegan upbringing. And I don't enjoy spending most of my free time in the kitchen. But I love eating tasty and healthy foods. Therefore, I prepare anything I feel like eating in a vegan, healthy way. Believe me, every single dish can be veganized. In the last two years I've learned how to make plant-based, healthy, and homemade Caesar salad, tartare steak, spaghetti a la carbonara, mousse au chocolate, and many others.

If you don't know how to make super-healthy homemade burgers or ice cream, just buy them from a nearby health food store or order them online. Anyway, they will be healthier than the main street, non-vegan ones. The more your child is opposed to change, the more you need to show them that they can still enjoy their favorite foods as vegans. And if your child is an explorer, there are plenty of new foods and cuisines to introduce them to – Chinese, Thai, Indian, Arab, as well as Greek and Italian.

Presentation

How food looks and smells is always important. The good news is that plant-based foods tend to look and smell much better than the traditional ones. It is especially true in a preparation phase – just compare the looks and the smells of the raw vegan ingredients (vegetables, fruits and grains) with the non-vegan ones (meat, dairy, eggs).

Depending on your parenting style and your kids' preferences, you can engage them in the food preparation process or (if they're not interested) just serve them vegan plates that are colorful, tasty-looking, and smell delicious.

On a personal note: a game I've played with my children (and still do) is "a food rainbow" – we come up with various colors for salads or savory dishes, even if "black" means a partially burnt onion sometimes.

Choice

I believe choice is always the key in raising your child. Don't get me wrong – I'm not talking about letting your children do whatever they want. I'm talking about giving them a decision margin, which will allow them not only to learn how to make their own choices (within your household rules) but will also teach them to bear the consequences of their own choices. Kids (just like anybody else) like to be taken seriously and have their say. So if you show them you take their preferences into consideration, they will appreciate it. In this case we're talking about food choices. Since you want to give your child healthy, plant-based foods, these should be the only foods that you buy and keep in your pantry and fridge. So if your kid wants a snack, they can choose from a range of healthy, vegan snacks. The same goes for main courses, desserts, etc.

Since you are in charge, you can make sure that whatever your child chooses, it will be a healthy choice.

Healthy cuisine

There are a lot of dietary theories out there and it can get quite confusing. Let me tell you what I believe to be the only truly healthy way of eating – first, eating vegan, second, eating a variety, and third, eating whole foods – which means eating non-processed whole foods of plant origin. So the diet I recommend is one of the variations of plant-based whole food or vegan whole food eating. I have already explained why vegan; now let me explain why whole foods are important.

I'll start with a simple example – an apple. You can eat the whole fruit (leaving just its core) or you can juice it. Let's compare both – the whole apple and freshly squeezed apple juice (I won't talk about the pasteurized juice made from concentrate standing on a shop shelf for months, since it has very little nutritional value, if any). When you juice your apple, you throw away fiber contained in its peel and pulp. What you get is basically water with lots of fruit sugar and some vitamins.

When you eat the whole apple, you get easily absorbed vitamins, water and fiber in perfect proportions. The best way to consume our apple would be to eat it unpeeled since its peel contains more fiber and micronutrients than its flesh. Eating apples has been proven to reduce cholesterol levels, promote keeping an appropriate body weight, and also reduce the risk of many diseases such as certain types of cancer, cardiovascular diseases, irritable bowel syndrome, and diabetes. Also, the bare act of biting and chewing the apple promotes healthy teeth and gums. Moreover, our mouth is the beginning of our digestive tract and chewing on our food provides our brain with information about what we're eating and therefore assures that the appropriate enzymes will get released in order to digest it. None of these processes takes place when you drink apple juice (even homemade, freshly squeezed juice).

The same goes for other foods. If we take grains, for example, a whole grain consists of bran (a peel), germ (a plant embryo) and endosperm (a food store for the developing plant embryo). When we refine grains – such as when converting brown rice into white rice or wheat into couscous – 80 percent of the nutrients and fiber get removed together with the bran and germ. So it's essential to eat whole foods as often as you can.

The process of food preparation is also important for nutrient values. When you cook grains or vegetables, some of their nutrients will dissolve in the cooking water. So I recommend not pouring it out, but using it to cook other things.

When I cook grains, I rinse them thoroughly in a strainer first. (If I don't have one, I just pour cold water on them, mix and then pour the water out and I repeat it until the water gets quite clear.) And then I add just as much water as I believe they will absorb – no more. I boil them for several minutes and then turn the heat off and leave them covered. After some time, I check if they are cooked and absorbed all the water. If they're still not done, I add some more water and boil them for some minutes again. The perfectly-cooked grains are not burned on the bottom: they are soft, and usually there are a few small gaps between the grains on the surface.

As far as vegetable preparation goes, I sometimes steam or simmer them with a little water or water and olive oil, and then I use the water to serve them in or to prepare a sauce. As I mentioned above, when I cook vegetables such as peeled potatoes or green beans, I use the cooking water. I keep it in the fridge and on the same day or the next day I use it instead of tap water to cook soup.

Vegan (on a) budget
A lot of people ask me about the costs of a vegan lifestyle versus a traditional one. I say there's no difference. You can spend a lot of money or a little money on food as a vegan just as you can when eating a diet that includes animal products.

However, when you look at food prices, you can see that animal products (such as meat, poultry, fish, seafood, and cheese) are usually much more expensive than vegan ones (such as vegetables, fruits, and grains or cereals). Of course, there are some expensive plant-based products on the market, especially organic and ready-made ones, but the same is true for animal products.

Therefore I believe that a cost of food is more lifestyle than diet-related. I say that the more food you prepare from scratch, the less you have to pay for it – which, again, is true for any kind of diet. Of course, it takes time, but in addition to saving money, it allows you to be in control of what you eat. Cooking at home, you can assure that your food is the best quality. You're in charge not only of your menu, but also of all the ingredients and their processing. In the end, the time you spend preparing meals will result in high-quality, healthy food for little money.

So, if you're a vegan on a budget, I advise you to forget about the ready-made foods and to prepare as much of your food as you can yourself using simple ingredients. This means you should have lots of grains, dried beans, seeds and nuts in your pantry. Apart from these staples, you'll need vegetable oils, herbs, spices and condiments. Then you only need to buy fresh vegetables and fruits — and you're all set.

Believe me, you can prepare everything you need from scratch, including foods like tofu and plant-based milks. I've been there and done it all. However, I'll be the first person to understand if you don't want to spend all your time in the kitchen. As much as I love to eat well, I don't like to spend much time cooking. If you are like me, you want to make all the time you spend preparing food worthwhile.

Still, there are lots of tricks to make your kitchen time worthwhile and to economize it together with your money. Here are some of my tips:

First of all, plan your menu ahead of time. If you have to provide food for seven days a week, think about repeating some dishes or at least using the leftovers on the next day.

Second, buy in bulk and prepare in bulk. Don't worry if you cook or prepare too much of something – you can always freeze it and use it for the same dish or a variation later. (It helps to label what you've frozen.)

Third, cook your grains just in water (don't add salt). Then you can use them for both savory and sweet dishes.

Fourth, and very important, look for versatile dishes. For example, if you make a soup – let's say a vegetable broth, it can get boring the next day, so mix it up by adding new ingredients and/or spices like tomatoes and basil, or mushrooms, or spinach and garlic, and then you've got a completely new soup. If you make a paté, you can also use it as a spread for sandwiches or fry or bake thick slices of it and serve them as plant-based cutlets. If you buy potatoes, you can cook some of them in their peels, and make mashed potatoes, and the next day you can peel the leftovers to prepare a potato salad, and if some are still left, you can make homemade potato patties, etc.

Fifth, use leftovers. If you cooked too much of the vegetables, beans, or grains, just mix them together with spices and you've got a perfect pulp to make patties, burgers or paté. If you don't have enough for this purpose, or don't feel like doing it at the moment, freeze them and use them up in the next few days.

The same goes for fruits. Let me give you an example: I prepare loads of apple sauce for my kids' breakfasts in winter – I serve it hot with millet in the mornings. But once they're fed up with it and ask for something else, I add whole meal flakes and nuts and make an apple crumble or use it as a cake ingredient. Cereals are probably the most versatile ingredient – you can add them to virtually anything savory — soup, burgers, salads, patés, etc., and you add them to sweet things: pancakes, cakes, puddings, pralines and so on.

Sixth, be creative. I find that my imagination is the only limit in plant-based cuisine. Even after many years, I'm still learning. Let me give you some examples of vegan counterparts to non-vegan staple foods I've learned to prepare in recent months: a plant-based "lard with cracklings" spread made of white beans and fried onions; a vegan "cheesecake" made of millet; plant-based "mac & cheese" sauce made of potatoes and carrots; a vegan marzipan made of potatoes and almonds; a plant-based meringue made out of aquafaba (chickpea cooking water); and also an avocado-based chocolate mousse. While it may look like I'm learning to prepare more desserts than savory dishes, my point is that there are no limits – it's just a matter of your culinary imagination... and some spices. Spice up your life!

Shopping

The basis of a healthy vegan diet is whole grains, vegetables, fruits, beans, seeds and nuts.

Whole grains: millet; red, black or brown rice (long, rounded, basmati); bulgur, buckwheat (white and toasted), barley, quinoa, teff, wild rice, whole oat meal, whole-meal flours (wheat, rice, rye, buckwheat, barley, millet); whole-meal pasta and bread, etc.

Vegetables and fruits: it's best to buy them fresh, seasonal, and locally grown. Getting the organically-grown ones would be ideal. But as long as they're fresh it's all good. I won't list them, since there are thousands of edible fruits and vegetables in the world. I just recommend that you not limit your menu to a few favorite ones, but to "eat rainbow" instead; and not forget about consuming leafy greens daily, which is indispensable to your health. The rest depends on availability, season, and your preferences. I encourage you to buy fresh vegetables and fruits from your local suppliers whenever you can. The ideal would be to go to the local farmers' market every other day, but not everybody can do so. I can't, so what I do is go to my local vegetable and fruit store and look at the selection and prices. They usually display the country of origin, and if I'm not sure, I ask them if it is a season for a particular product and if they're locally grown.

Beans: red, white, pinto, chickpeas, soy, lentils of all colors, etc. – better buy the dried ones, than those that are canned or jarred.

Seeds and nuts: sunflower, flax, pumpkin, chia, hemp, sesame, almonds, coconut, cashew, hazel, macadamia, pistachios, etc. Buy unsalted and non-toasted ones.

You will also need some oils. Look for the cold-pressed ones. To prepare hot dishes, oils with a high smoking point are the most appropriate. I use an extra virgin cold-pressed olive oil for cooking or frying and a virgin coconut oil for baking and preparing desserts. Low smoke point cold-pressed oils – for example safflower, flax, walnut, and sunflower – are the best to use in salads, dips and other cold dishes.

Then you only need herbs and spices. Look for fresh ones, like garlic, onion, basil, rosemary, and coriander. You can also buy dried herbs and spices – just look for the ones with natural ingredients– such as a mixture of dried spices and herbs, a mix of peppers and curry. Avoid the ones containing salt, sugar, or artificial colorants. Red sweet pepper and smoked pepper, oregano, turmeric, ginger, cinnamon, and other dried herbs can also be useful.

There are some little processed foods that are still very healthy. Let's start with soy products such as tempeh and tofu. The other often underestimated group are naturally fermented foods such as miso, kimchi (make sure it's vegan), sauerkraut, and pickled vegetables (you need to make sure they don't contain vinegar – just vegetables, salt and spices), and soy sauce (make sure it was naturally brewed and contains only soy, salt and maybe some grains). The natural fermentation process of preserving foods in salty water makes them easier to digest and provides our intestines with friendly bacteria. It can also raise the vitamin levels in them – especially the vitamin C.

As I said above, the ideal is to buy only organically and locally grown foods. It's not always possible, since they are not always available and sometimes are pricey. I encourage you to buy them as often as you can (especially if you're feeding them to the babies). Sometimes the price difference between an organic and non-organic product is very small (for example potatoes, apples, onions, whole grains, whole-meal flours and pasta, cold-pressed oils, seasonings); in this case, I would go for those that were farmed organically.

Also, it's important in the case of foods that are often GMO, such as soy or corn and their products: if GMO is not reliably labelled in your country, buying products with an organic certificate assures that they don't contain any GMOs. Organic origin is also important, if you want to use unpeeled fruits and vegetables – for example, if you need a lemon or orange peel in your desserts – make sure these are organically grown lemons. Some fruits like apples are healthier when consumed unpeeled. If you can't buy organically grown apples, you can at least buy the unwaxed ones – I often buy these for my sons – I just wash them and cut them into pieces and put them in my sons' lunchboxes alongside with their plant-based sandwiches to provide them with a healthy snack.

To sum it up: you need to buy unprocessed, vegan foods. Avoid highly-processed, ready-made convenience foods. And of course, and most importantly, avoid all foods of animal origin such as meat, poultry, fish, seafood, milk, cheese, yoghurt, cream, butter, eggs, gelatin, honey, etc. The ideal would be to buy single ingredients and prepare your food from scratch. However, when you need to buy foods containing several ingredients, just read the ingredients list carefully. The shorter the list, the better. You also need to be careful with food additives – some of them are not vegan and some of them can be harmful for your health.

I've been checking ingredients lists for 27 years now and I can tell you, it's much more fun doing it together with your kids. I remember all three of them reading out loud in the shops, when they were still learning to read. My twin sons usually made it a competition. Some words were long and difficult, and we had to discuss their meaning. It not only helped to ground their vegan identity, but it was also a good excuse to talk about healthy food and food processing (including checking what E symbols mean and whether the foods are vegan). Later on, my sons acted as detectives looking for non-vegan ingredients. They still check if what we buy is vegan, and nowadays I'm very grateful for this, especially when the print is small.

5 Bright future

Raising a child can be a demanding task. And raising a vegan child in a non-vegan society often seems even more complicated. But let's face it – you have no choice if you want to give your child the best. And on the other hand, it is a very satisfying process.

You can see your child growing healthy. I am not saying that vegan kids never get sick. But on the average, they are healthier than their omnivorous peers. They get sick more rarely and recover faster; they have fewer allergies; and they are never obese. (Speaking from experience, my 12-year-old twin sons have never taken an antibiotic or had a broken bone.) Vegan upbringing is also an investment in their healthy future – they won't be at risk of obesity, diabetes, heart disease and many other civilization diseases.

And you should not forget about the fact that you are shaping the vanguard of a future society. I have no doubt that veganism is the only possible future for our society and our planet. The revolution has already started, and we – the parents of the vegan generation – are playing an important role in it.

Vegan children do not receive a popular double-standard education (that is, we love cats and dogs, but we turn a blind eye to the suffering of other species), and therefore they grow up much more conscious, compassionate, and ethics-oriented than the average child (not to mention our generation). They also benefit from their non-standard upbringing by being more self-aware and by thinking out of the box. Seeing you as their role model, they learn to justify and defend their opinions and choices early in life.

So be assured that you are on the best path for raising a healthy, happy, independent, compassionate human being. Congratulations and good luck!

6 Further reading

I wrote this chapter for readers who want to dig deeper into the topic. If you are still hesitant about raising your child vegan, I hope it will help you make up your mind. And I hope it can also help you when you feel the need to support your decision with scientific facts, for example when you defend it in a discussion with someone who might be skeptical.

A side note: I believe nowadays you can find evidence online supporting any claim you can make. Our (consumers') minds are a battlefield for various industries and producers. To put it straight, everyone wants to sell you on their product. It's up to you to decide what products (and therefore lifestyle) you'll get sold on. If you don't make a decision, you are still making one – you're just going along with the mainstream. So if you want to find the facts online, look for articles based on independent scientific studies.

I include a list of things I recommend reading and watching here. Of course, this is not a complete list – there are hundreds (if not thousands) of documents, studies, articles, etc., available online, and I've just picked up the ones that caught my interest and which are based in fact.

Many of them link to the T. Colin Campbell Center for Nutrition Studies. Why? There are two reasons. First, Professor Thomas Colin Campbell was one of the leading scientists of what has come to be known as the China Study – the largest-scale and most comprehensive nutrition study conducted so far. I learned of this study in 2000 when I was head of a Polish division of a vegan NGO; it was our point of scientific reference. Second, I graduated from that center.

I also list quite a few links to The Physicians Committee for Responsible Medicine (PCRM). This is a non-profit research and advocacy organization based in Washington DC, which promotes a vegan diet and preventive medicine.

Let me just warn you here – there will be a lot of talk in these articles about diseases and serious health conditions, and in some of the videos, there is some graphic violence. The reason for these "scare tactics" is that nobody (in their right mind) would question the health benefits of eating vegetables, fruits, beans and grains, and therefore, when discussing the health benefits of veganism, experts tend to focus more on the negative impact on human health of consuming animal products.

I've organized these resources by the following themes: why a vegan diet is optimal health-wise; why a plant-based diet is optimal for children at any stage of their lives; why milk and dairy products are bad for your health; why fish and seafood are bad for your health; why you shouldn't rely on vitamins and supplements; why being vegan is good for the environment.

Why a vegan diet is optimal health-wise

https://www.vegansociety.com/go-vegan/health (the Vegan Society is a registered charity and the oldest vegan society in the world, founded in the UK in November 1944. The link sums up the health benefits of the vegan diet.)

https://nutritionstudies.org/the-china-study/ (The China Study)

https://www.wellandgood.com/good-food/china-study-cheat-sheet-10-things-you-need-to-know/ (This is the China Study in a nutshell.)

https://www.livekindly.co/vegan-doctor-michael-klaper-nasa/amp/ (Michael A. Klaper is an American physician, vegan health educator, and conference and event speaker, and the author of articles and books of vegan medical advice.)

Why a vegan diet is optimal for children at any stage of their lives

https://www.pcrm.org/good-nutrition/plant-based-diets/pregnancy

https://www.pcrm.org/good-nutrition/nutrition-for-kids

https://nutritionstudies.org/why-parents-should-keep-children-meat-and-dairy-free/ (The iconic Dr Spock talking on children' health)

Why milk and dairy products are bad for your health

https://nutritionstudies.org/no-body-needs-milk/

https://nutritionstudies.org/12-frightening-facts-milk/

https://www.pcrm.org/good-nutrition/nutrition-information/health-concerns-about-dairy

https://www.pcrm.org/news/news-releases/doctors-urge-2020-2025-dietary-guidelines-advisory-committee-ditch-dairy

Why fish and seafood are bad for your health

https://nutritionstudies.org/fish-part-healthy-diet/

https://www.peta.org/living/food/think-fish-health-food/_(People for the Ethical Treatment of Animals is an American non-profit corporation with nearly 400 employees founded in 1980.)

https://mercyforanimals.org/4-reasons-seafood-isnt-as-healthy-as-you

Why you shouldn't rely on vitamins and supplements to provide healthy nutrition

https://nutritionstudies.org/vitamins-supplements/

Why being vegan is good for the environment and therefore for the future of our planet

http://humanefacts.org/infographic/

https://nutritionstudies.org/impact-of-food-choices-on-the-environment/

https://www.vegansociety.com/go-vegan/environment

https://www.peta.org.uk/blog/how-going-vegan-helps-stop-climate-change/

https://www.ft.com/content/3b210ddc-bba0-11e8-8274-55b72926558f

https://www.theguardian.com/environment/2018/may/31/avoiding-meat-and-dairy-is-single-biggest-way-to-reduce-your-impact-on-earth

https://www.independent.co.uk/life-
style/health-and-families/veganism-
environmental-impact-planet-reduced-plant-
based-diet-humans-study-a8378631.html

https://www.pcrm.org/news/health-
nutrition/substituting-beans-beef-beneficial-
environment

https://www.pcrm.org/news/health-
nutrition/vegetarian-diets-best-environment-
and-human-health

https://www.plantbasednews.org/post/5-
surprising-facts-about-veganism-and-the-
planet-on-world-environment-day

There are also documentaries explaining the health benefits of veganism, which you can watch or recommend: "Forks Over Knives," "What the Health," "Cowspiracy", "The Game Changers" and many more. And there is also a famous movie on animal exploitation called "Earthlings," narrated by Joaquin Phoenix and featuring music by Moby (both of whom are not only longtime vegans but also animal rights activists).

Made in the USA
Columbia, SC
22 August 2021

44110111R00076